Around the World in Eighty Days

by Jules Verne

CEFR level A2

Adapted by Karen Kovacs
for
Read Stories – Learn English

Read Stories – Learn English

Around the World in Eighty Days: CEFR level A2 (ELT Graded Reader)
Original text by Jules Verne
Adapted text © Karen Kovacs, 2025
Illustrations by Alphonse de Neuville and Léon Benett
Logo © Karen Kovacs, 2025

No part of this book may be reproduced, scanned or distributed in any printed or electronic form without permission. Please do not participate in or encourage piracy of copyrighted materials in violation of the author's rights. Thank you for respecting the hard work of the author.

CONTENTS

What are graded readers?   Page 4

Meet the author   Page 5

People in the story   Page 7

The story   Page 9

Exercises   Page 93

More stories   Page 94

Words from the story   Page 96

WHAT ARE GRADED READERS?

Graded readers are books in easy English. They are written for learners of English and use **vocabulary and grammar at your level**.

Each book also includes some new, more difficult words. There are **definitions** for these words at the back of the book.

WHY READ GRADED READERS?

- Studies show that learners who read in English **improve in all areas much faster** than learners who don't read.

- You **don't need a dictionary** so reading is **relaxing**.

- The stories are all in **modern English**.

- You learn vocabulary and grammar **in context** (this is the best way, according to teachers).

- Reading a book in English improves your **comprehension, fluency** and **confidence**.

- Graded readers are not exercises. They are **real stories** you can enjoy, helping you **learn English naturally**.

Meet
the author

My name is Karen.

- I'm a writer from England.
- I'm the winner of a Language Learner Literature Award.
- I have a Degree in English Literature and a Master's in Linguistics.
- I'm an experienced English teacher, in the UK and abroad.
- I speak Hungarian, French and Spanish, so I understand how it feels to learn a new language!

Karen Kovacs

ReadStories-LearnEnglish.com

More stories at the same level

New words

When you see a word in **bold**, go to the back of the book. There you will find a definition of the word.

People in the story

Phileas Fogg

Passepartout – Fogg's **servant**

Detective Fix

Aouda – a young Indian woman

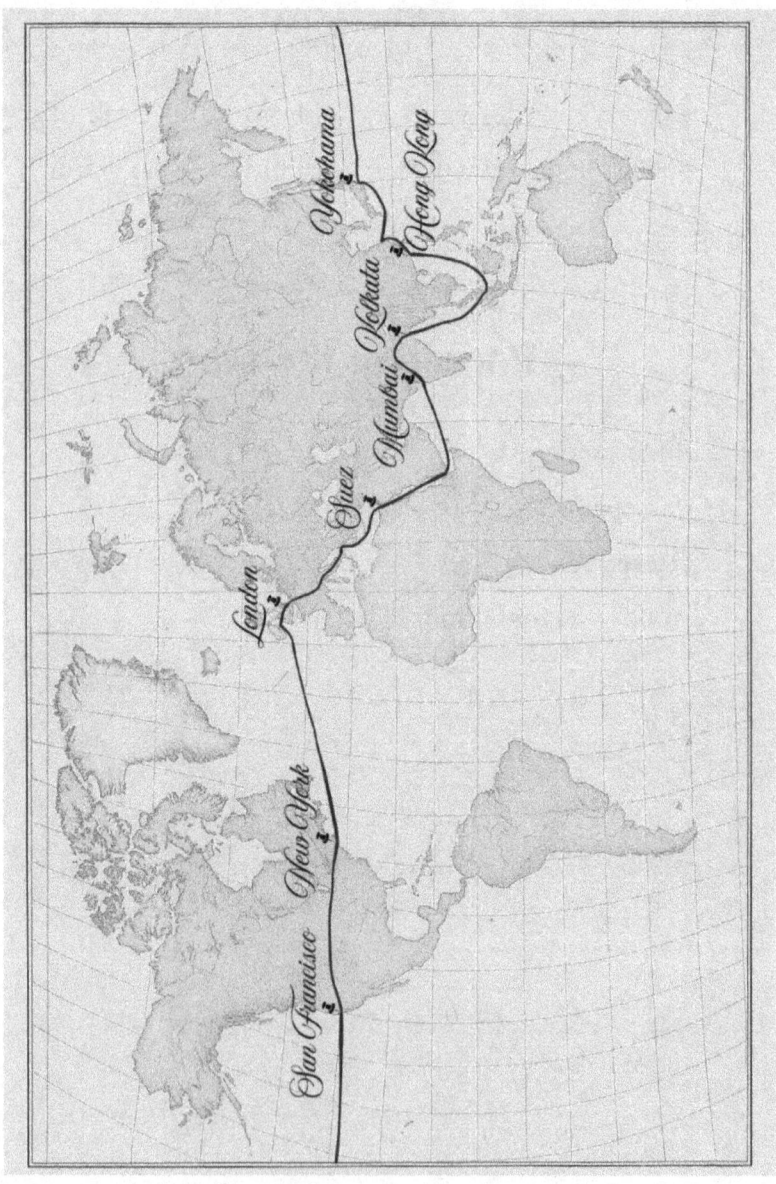

Chapter 1
Phileas Fogg meets Passepartout

Mr Phileas Fogg lived, in 1872, at Number 7 Saville Row, London. He was a member of the Reform Club, a special place for important men. They met to talk, eat and relax together.

Did Phileas Fogg have a job? No. But was he rich? Yes. Nobody knew where his money came from.

He was a very quiet man. His only hobbies were reading the newspaper and playing whist, a card game. He knew a lot about the world but he didn't travel anymore. These days, he stayed in London.

Phileas Fogg didn't have a wife or children, but this isn't very unusual. However, he also had no good friends or family, and this is more unusual.

He lived alone and ate his meals alone at the Reform Club at exactly the same time every day.

Fogg's life was simple and he had only one servant. One day, on 2 October, his **servant**, James Forster, brought him water for washing. Unfortunately, the water was thirty-eight degrees, not forty. Because of this, Fogg said, "You must leave my house immediately. I'll find a new servant."

Later that morning, Phileas Fogg sat in his chair and waited for his new servant. He watched his clock, which showed the hours, minutes and seconds. It was nearly half past ten, the time he normally went to the Reform Club.

At that moment, a young man, about thirty years old, entered the room.

"Are you John?" Phileas Fogg asked.

"It's Jean," answered the man. "Jean Passepartout."

"You're French," said Fogg.

"Yes," said Passepartout. "I've had several different jobs, Mr Fogg. I worked in a **circus** for a few years and, before that, I was a singer and a dancer. I left France five years ago and became a servant. I want a quiet life now, you see."

"Alright," said Fogg. "From this moment, twenty-nine minutes past ten, you are my servant."

Passepartout looked at his new **master**. Fogg was about forty years old, with a handsome face and a

beard. He never hurried and never showed emotion.

Passepartout had a pleasant face, with blue eyes and brown hair. He was strong and rounder than the Englishman. He was kind and funny.

Phileas Fogg stood up and, without another word,

left for the Reform Club.

Passepartout stayed in the house alone. He looked around and saw that everything was clean and tidy.

He smiled. "My new master lives a quiet life. That's perfect for me! I've had enough adventure."

Chapter 2
An expensive conversation

Phileas Fogg arrived at the Reform Club. He went to the dining room and sat at the same table he always sat at. He ate his breakfast and drank several cups of tea. Then he stood up and went to the large hall. There, a member of staff brought him The Times newspaper and he read it until a quarter to one. He had lunch, then read some other newspapers.

Half an hour later, other members of the Reform Club came in and sat by the fire. They were Fogg's whist partners. They were all rich, important men.

"Have you heard about the **robbery**?" asked Thomas Flanagan, a businessman. "A man stole fifty-five thousand pounds! Everyone is talking about it!"

"The bank will lose the money," said Andrew Stuart, an engineer.

"No!" said Gauthier Ralph, a manager of the Bank of England. "**Detectives** are looking for the **robber**. They'll find him, I'm sure!"

"How did it happen?"

"Someone took the money from a desk at the bank." Phileas Fogg spoke these words from behind his newspaper. He put it down and joined the conversation. "If a detective finds the robber and the money, the bank will give him two thousand pounds."

"Where can the robber go?" asked Ralph.

"The world is a big place," said Stuart.

"It was but it's not so big anymore," said Phileas Fogg, starting his card game with Flanagan.

"Has the world got smaller?" Stuart laughed.

"Yes, it has!" answered Ralph. "I agree with Mr Fogg. The world is smaller because now we can travel around it ten times faster than a hundred years ago."

But Stuart didn't agree. "Maybe you can go around the world in three months now, but that doesn't mean—"

"In eighty days," said Phileas Fogg.

"That's true," said Ralph. "In India, there is a new railway between Kholby and Prayagraj. So now it's possible to travel around the world in eighty days. I read about it in the Daily Telegraph. Look!"

He showed the page in the newspaper:

London to Suez (Egypt)... 7 days
Suez to Mumbai (India)... 13 days
Mumbai to Kolkata (India)... 3 days
Kolkata to Hong Kong... 13 days
Hong Kong to Yokohama (Japan)... 6 days
Yokohama to San Francisco... 22 days
San Francisco to New York... 7 days
New York to London... 9 days
Total... 80 days

"But what about bad weather or accidents?" said Stuart.

"That is all included," said Phileas Fogg, without looking up from his cards.

"Why don't you do it then?" asked Stuart.

"I'm happy to do it," said Fogg.

"That's crazy!" said Stuart. Then he thought for a moment. "If you try it, I'll **bet** four thousand pounds that it's impossible."

"Alright," said Fogg. He looked at the others, who were all listening. "I've got twenty thousand pounds in the bank. If I can't go around the world in eighty days, that money is yours."

"Twenty thousand pounds!" shouted Flanagan. "If you're late at all, we'll win twenty thousand pounds!"

"I won't be late," said Phileas Fogg quietly. "Does anyone else want to bet against me?"

Ralph, Stuart, Flanagan and two others, Samuel Fallentin and John Sullivan, discussed it for a few minutes. They all agreed to bet a total of twenty thousand pounds.

"Good," said Fogg. "The train leaves for Dover at a quarter to nine. I'll be on it."

"This evening?" asked Stuart, surprised.

"Yes," answered Fogg. "Today is Wednesday, 2 October. I must return here, to the Reform Club, on Saturday, 21 December, at a quarter to nine in the evening. If I don't, my money belongs to you."

Phileas Fogg had forty thousand pounds so he was betting half his money. He needed the other half to complete this difficult journey.

"When I get back to London," he explained, "you can look at my passport. The **stamps** from each country will show you that I was really there."

It was seven o'clock.

"Let's stop playing so you can prepare for your trip," said the others.

"No," said Fogg. "I'm ready. Let's finish the game."

Chapter 3

Passepartout is surprised

Phileas Fogg won twenty pounds at whist, said goodbye to his friends and, at twenty-five minutes past seven, left the Reform Club.

When he arrived home, Passepartout was surprised to see him. "You're very early," he said.

"We're leaving for Dover in ten minutes," said Fogg.

Passepartout didn't understand. "Where are you going?"

"We're going around the world," said Fogg.

The servant's mouth opened. He held up his hands and almost fell to the floor.

"Around the world?" he said.

"In eighty days," answered Fogg. "We have to leave this evening."

"But what about the suitcases?"

"We don't need any. Pack a small bag with a few shirts, my coat and my walking shoes. We'll buy clothes on the journey."

Passepartout tried to speak but no words came out. Instead, he went upstairs and fell into a chair. "I wanted a quiet life!" he thought.

By eight o'clock, both men were ready. Fogg took a small book with all the timetables for the world's railways and **steamships**.

Passepartout was holding a bag and Fogg put some money into it.

"Be careful," Fogg said. "The bag has twenty thousand pounds in it."

Passepartout was so surprised that he couldn't speak.

They left the house and took a taxi to Charing Cross station. The night was dark and it was raining.

Before they went inside, they saw a poor woman with a child in her arms. Both were thin and dirty, and it was clear that they lived on the streets.

Fogg took the twenty pounds he won at whist and gave it to the woman.

Passepartout watched and thought, "My master has a warm heart."

They got into the train **carriage** and watched from the window while the train moved slowly out of the station.

After Paris, they travelled across France and Italy, then got on the steamship *Mongolia* at Brindisi. This took them to Suez in Egypt.

The news of Phileas Fogg's journey was now in all the newspapers. Everyone was talking about it and most people thought it was impossible.

In Suez, a man called Detective Fix waited for the *Mongolia*. He believed that Fogg was the bank robber. A worker at the bank described someone exactly like him, and Fogg left London very quickly after the robbery. For Fix, it was clear that Fogg didn't want the police to find him.

The detective laughed to himself. "When Fogg arrives, I'll **arrest** him. Then I'll get the two-thousand-pound prize money."

At eleven o'clock on Wednesday, 9 October, the *Mongolia* arrived in Suez and its passengers began to leave the ship. Fix watched carefully. Which one was Phileas Fogg?

One of the passengers came to ask Fix a question. "Excuse me," he said, "where can I get a stamp for this passport?"

Fix looked at the passport. It was Phileas Fogg's!

"Is this yours?" he asked.

"No, it's my master's," said the man.

"Where is your master?"

"He stayed on the ship. It goes to Mumbai in four hours so he doesn't need to get off."

As soon as Passepartout left, Fix sent a message to the police station in London:

"I've found the bank robber. His name is Phileas Fogg. Send a **warrant** to Mumbai."

Chapter 4
Passepartout talks too much

Detective Fix met Passepartout again and started a friendly conversation.

"Did Mr Fogg get the stamp for his passport?" he asked.

"Yes," said Passepartout. "Now I'm going to look around the town. My master isn't interested – he prefers to stay in his room on the ship. Are we really in Egypt?"

"Yes," said Fix.

"In Africa?"

"Yes."

"Africa!" said Passepartout, **amazed**. "I can't believe I'm in Africa! We're travelling so fast – it's like a dream."

Fix smiled. "Are you hurrying then, on this journey around the world?"

"I'm not hurrying but my master is."

"Where are you going?"

"Around the world in eighty days!"

"Really?" said the detective. "And your master – is he rich?"

"Oh yes," said Passepartout. "He's carrying a lot of money in his bag and he doesn't mind spending it. He's

going to give the **captain** of the *Mongolia* a big **reward** if we get to Mumbai early."

"I see," said Fix. "And do you know your master well?"

"No!" answered Passepartout. "I only started working for him the day we left London."

Fix listened carefully. With every answer, he was more sure that Fogg was the robber. He left London quickly, carrying lots of cash and hurrying from one place to the next.

"Oh, I just remembered – I must buy shoes and shirts."

"I can show you some good shops," said Fix kindly.

"Thank you!" said Passepartout, and they walked into busy town together.

"Is Mumbai far from here?" asked Passepartout while they walked.

"Yes, quite far. It's ten days by sea."

"And what country is it in?"

"India."

"In Asia?"

"Yes."

Fix bought a ticket for the *Mongolia* too. He wanted to follow Fogg to India, which was a British country. When the warrant arrived there, Fix could arrest Fogg.

The steamship left Suez and moved through the Red Sea. Fogg spent most of his time in his room, reading and writing the details of his trip in a little notebook – the times and dates.

When the sea became **rough**, he didn't worry that the ship might be late. Phileas Fogg was always **calm**.

Passepartout enjoyed the journey. He often walked around the ship and talked to other passengers. On the second day, he saw someone he knew.

"Ah! Hello, Mr Fix!" he said happily. He still didn't know that Fix was a detective. "You're going to Mumbai too!"

"Yes, that's right," said Fix. "How is Mr Fogg?"

"Very well," said Passepartout. "He eats three good meals a day in his room and plays whist with other passengers."

After that, the detective and the servant chatted every day. The weather was warm and they were now on the Indian Ocean.

On Sunday, 20 October, at noon, the passengers saw India for the first time. Four hours later, the ship arrived in Mumbai.

They were two days early. Fogg wrote this information in his notebook.

Chapter 5

A problem on the railway

India is a very big country, more than three million square kilometres. At that time, Britain **controlled** most of it but some parts of the country were still free.

India was changing fast. Before, people travelled on foot or by horse. Now, steamboats moved quickly on the Indus and the Ganges rivers, and a new railway crossed the country from Mumbai to Kolkata (also called Calcutta) in only three days.

The passengers from the *Mongolia* left the ship at half past four in the afternoon. The train to Kolkata was **due** to leave at exactly eight.

Mr Fogg said goodbye to his whist partners and went to the passport office to get his stamp. He wasn't interested in Mumbai, its famous city hall, beautiful library, markets or **holy** buildings.

Afterwards, he went to the railway station and ate dinner there.

Detective Fix went to the Mumbai police station and

told them about the bank robbery.

"Has the warrant for Mr Fogg's arrest arrived?" he asked.

"No, it hasn't," said the policeman.

Passepartout was really enjoying himself. He watched dancers dressed in gold and silver, then walked through the busy streets.

He started walking to the railway station. But he passed a beautiful temple and wanted to look inside.

He didn't know that it was **against the law** to go into Indian temples, if you were a Christian, and it was also against the law to go in with shoes.

Passepartout walked in like a simple tourist and was amazed by the colours and lights. It was so beautiful. But **suddenly**, three **priests** ran to him, shouting. They were very angry. They pulled his shoes from his feet and hit him.

Passepartout hit them back and then ran out of the temple as fast as possible, but without his shoes.

At five minutes to eight, he arrived at the station.

Fix was following him and heard when Passepartout explained to his master about the problem in the

temple.

"I hope this will not happen again," said Fogg coldly, and he got onto the train.

Poor Passepartout followed his master, feeling very sad.

Detective Fix watched them but didn't follow. He

couldn't leave India until the warrant arrived from London.

A moment later, the train gave a long **whistle** and moved away into the night.

During the journey, Phileas Fogg **worked out** the number of hours since they left London, and he wrote the answer in his notebook.

The train passed an island and some mountains. The next day, it passed lots of little villages and farms, where people grew coffee and black-pepper plants.

Later, they saw a jungle full of wild animals – snakes, elephants and tigers.

The next day, the train suddenly stopped.

"Passengers must get out here!" shouted a railway worker.

"What do you mean?" asked Fogg. "Why have we stopped?"

"The railway isn't finished," the man explained.

"What?" said Passepartout. He felt more worried than Fogg, who was calm as usual.

"There is no railway yet between here and Prayagraj," said the man. "The railway begins there again."

"But the newspapers said that the railway was ready," said Fogg.

"Well, the newspapers were wrong," the man answered, walking away. This was lucky for him because Passepartout wanted to hit him!

Chapter 6
Riding on an elephant

"This railway problem will delay us a lot!" said Passepartout.

"I **expected** it," said Fogg calmly.

"You knew about this?"

"Not at all," answered Fogg. "But I knew that, during our journey around the world, we were sure to have some problems. We arrived in Suez two days early so we can lose those days now. The steamship for Hong Kong leaves Kolkata at noon on the 25th. Today is only the 22nd. We have enough time."

"But how will we get to Prayagraj?" asked Passepartout.

"We'll walk," said Fogg.

Passepartout didn't like that idea so he went to talk to people in the village. Soon, he ran back.

"I've found an elephant!"

"An elephant?" said Fogg.

"Yes! It belongs to an Indian man from the village."

quicker that way."

It wasn't comfortable on Kiouni's back but nobody **complained**. A few times, Passepartout took a piece of sugar from his pocket and gave it to Kiouni, who was

"Let's go and see [...]

The Indian man sho[...] Kiouni.

Fogg wanted to rent it for [...] the man said no. For twenty po[...] Passepartout couldn't believe th[...] offering so much money!

"Then I'll buy the elephant," said Fo[gg...] take one thousand pounds?"

"No," said the man, his eyes bright and inte[...]

"Master, stop!" said Passepartout. "That i[s too] much!"

"I need that elephant to win the bet," explained Fogg. He looked at the Indian man again. "How about two thousand pounds?"

Finally, the man agreed.

"What a price!" shouted Passepartout.

They found a young Indian guide to travel with them. The guide climbed onto Kiouni's neck, Fogg sat on a seat at the animal's side and Passepartout climbed onto his back. At nine o'clock, they left the village.

"We'll go through the jungle," said the guide. "It's

very pleased.

After two hours, they stopped for an hour. The elephant was strong but needed a break and some food.

This was an area of India with very few people and no tourists. The British didn't control this part of the country. Through the trees, they sometimes saw some Indians but they weren't friendly. However, the monkeys were funny and Passepartout enjoyed their noisy games.

At eight in the evening, they stopped again.

"We've travelled forty kilometres," said Fogg. "Prayagraj is another forty kilometres."

The night air was cold and they were hungry. The guide made a small fire and they cooked some food. Kiouni ate from a large banana plant.

They slept under the stars and began again at six the next morning. The guide hoped to **reach** Prayagraj by evening.

Chapter 7

A dead man walks again

At four o'clock in the afternoon, the elephant suddenly stopped.

"What's wrong?" asked Passepartout.

The men listened. From far away, they heard some strange sounds in the jungle.

The guide went to look and soon came back. "A group of Brahmins are coming this way. They're Indian priests. They mustn't see us – they don't like foreign people near their holy places."

The group watched from behind some trees. The Brahmins walked along the path, singing and playing instruments. Two of them holding a young woman by the arms. She wore gold jewellery. The other men carried big knives.

When the group were gone, Fogg asked, "Where are they taking that woman?"

"Tomorrow morning, they'll **burn** her on a big fire until she is dead," said the guide.

"Burn her? Why?" asked Passepartout, suddenly very angry.

"Because her husband has died," explained the guide. "They'll burn his body and his wife must burn with him. It's against the law but, in this part of India, some people still do it."

"That's terrible," said Passepartout.

"Why didn't she run away?" asked Fogg.

"She can't," said the guide. "The Brahmins gave her **opium** so she can't walk without help. They're taking her to a temple about three kilometres from here."

Fogg thought for a moment. "We must **rescue** her."

The guide was surprised. "Rescue her, Mr Fogg?"

"Yes. I have an extra twelve hours. I'll use them for that."

Passepartout began to love his master. "You have such a good heart!" he said.

"Sometimes," answered the Englishman quietly. "When I have the time."

It was a dangerous plan. Fogg knew that the Brahmins might kill him but he wanted to try. And Passepartout was ready to help.

"The woman comes from a rich family," explained their guide, "and she speaks good English. Her name is Aouda."

They rode the elephant through the jungle until they were close to the temple. The night was dark and the sky was full of clouds.

"Let's go now!" said Passepartout.

"We can't," said their guide. "Look. She's inside the temple and there are men with knives next to her bed. They won't sleep tonight."

"Then we'll wait," said Fogg. "We may be able to rescue her later. I'm only due at Prayagraj by noon."

They waited. Passepartout was thinking and soon he had an idea. He didn't tell the others.

The night passed and morning came. The air filled with music and singing again. The temple doors opened and the Brahmins brought the woman out. Behind them came a large crowd.

The husband's body lay near the fire. Soon his wife must join him.

But suddenly, the singing stopped. The people began shouting and moving back, afraid.

The husband stood up! He took his wife in his arms and walked away from the fire.

The crowd couldn't believe it! And Fogg couldn't believe it.

When the husband reached Fogg, he said, "Let's go! Quickly!"

It was Passepartout.

It was still a bit dark so nobody saw when he lay down next to the fire. Then everyone believed he was the husband.

The guide brought the elephant. Fogg and Passepartout carried Aouda onto its back, and Kiouni took them quickly through the jungle.

The Brahmins finally understood that the real husband was still by the fire. They tried to find Fogg and the others but they were already far away.

Chapter 8
A problem in Kolkata

Aouda slept for a long time because of the opium. When she finally woke up, Fogg said, "You can't stay in India. It's too dangerous. The Brahmins will try to find you. Come with us to Hong Kong."

"Yes! I have an uncle there," Aouda said. "I can live with him."

At ten o'clock, they reached Prayagraj station, where the railway started again.

"What are you going to do with the elephant?" Passepartout asked Fogg.

Fogg thought for a moment. "You helped us a lot," he told the guide. "Would you like to keep the elephant?"

The guide smiled. "Oh, yes, please!"

They caught the train to Kolkata and arrived at seven the next morning. The steamship to Hong Kong was due to leave at noon.

"It's 25 October," he said. "This is exactly the day I

expected to reach Kolkata. We've lost no time."

But when they were leaving the station, a policeman stopped them.

"Mr Phileas Fogg?"

"Yes."

"And is that your servant?" He pointed to Passepartout.

"Yes."

"I've come to arrest you both. Please come with me."

Fogg didn't show any surprise and they all followed the policeman to a building on the town's main street.

Inside, a **judge** sat behind a desk. "Finally, we found you," he said.

Before he could explain, three Brahmin priests entered the room.

"They've arrested us because we rescued Aouda," Passepartout said quietly to Fogg.

The judge didn't hear him. "In Mumbai," he said to Passepartout, "you went into a temple."

"In Mumbai?" the Frenchman repeated. He almost didn't remember that.

"Yes. A man called Detective Fix told us about it."

Fix was sitting at the back of the room but the men didn't see him.

Another man stood up. "It's against the law for a foreign person to enter a temple. And look – we have your shoes! You wore them inside."

The judge spoke again. "You must go to prison for fifteen days, both you and your master."

Fix was very pleased. "Now Fogg will still be here when the warrant arrives," he thought.

Passepartout took Fogg's hands and said, "I'm so sorry, master. You're going to miss the steamship to Hong Kong because of me!"

"No, I won't," Fogg said calmly. Then he looked at the judge. "Can we pay a **fine** instead of going to prison?"

The judge was surprised. "Yes, but it's a very large fine."

"How much?"

"One thousand pounds... each."

"Alright," Fogg said. Fogg opened his bag, took out the money and gave it to the judge. "And please give back my servant's shoes."

Fix watched – very angry – while Fogg, the robber, left the room. There was nothing he could do.

It was now eleven o'clock. Fogg, Passepartout and Aouda took a taxi to the steamship *Rangoon*. They arrived **in time**.

During the journey, Aouda spent a lot of time with Fogg. He was polite and kind to her but he didn't talk much. She chatted to him and thanked him many times for rescuing her.

And where was Detective Fix? The others didn't know it but he was on the same ship.

"Britain controls Hong Kong too so the warrant will work there," he thought. "Maybe it will arrive before us."

The ship stopped at Singapore and then travelled across the South China Sea. Everything went well until a terrible storm hit the ship. For two days, the sea was very rough and the Rangoon could only move very slowly over the water.

This delayed them by twenty-four hours.

Fix was really pleased but Passepartout was angry. Aouda was amazed that Fogg wasn't worried but, of course, he expected problems like this.

On 4 November, however, the sea became calmer at last.

"It's good that the storm has ended," said Passepartout. "But now we'll miss the ship to Japan."

Fogg said nothing. He just checked his watch and wrote the time in his notebook.

Chapter 9

Plans in Hong Kong

They arrived in Hong Kong twenty-four hours late. When they got off the ship, they were surprised to see another one in the **harbour**. It was the *Carnatic*, the ship to Yokohama in Japan.

"Why hasn't it left?" Fogg asked the captain.

"There was a problem with the engine," the captain answered. "But they're repairing it now so we're leaving tomorrow morning."

Fogg was pleased. This gave them time to find Aouda's uncle. He booked three rooms at a hotel and then he and Aouda went into town.

Hong Kong belonged to Britain, and it was a busy place. People from China, Britain, France, America and Japan filled the streets, buying and selling things. While Fogg was with Aouda, Passepartout enjoyed walking around.

At the ticket office, he saw Detective Fix.

"Were you on the *Rangoon* too?" Passepartout

asked, surprised. "We didn't see you."

"Yes," said Fix. "I wasn't well so I stayed in my room."

Passepartout looked at him carefully. "I think he's following us," he thought, "probably because the men at the Reform Club sent him. They want to check that Mr Fogg is really going around the world. I won't tell my master – he'll be upset that his friends don't believe him."

"I suppose you're going to Yokohama next?" Fix asked.

"Yes," said Passepartout, "and then to America. Are you coming too?"

"Yes," said Fix but his face was angry. The warrant still wasn't there and Hong Kong was the last British country on Fogg's journey. If he couldn't arrest him there, he might lose the robber forever.

"I must try and keep Fogg in Hong Kong," he thought.

At that moment, the man at the ticket desk came with some news for them. "The *Carnatic* will leave this evening, not tomorrow morning," he said. "The repairs are finished."

Passepartout was excited. "I must tell my master!" he said.

Fix smiled. "Wait a minute, my friend. Let's have a drink first."

He took Passepartout to a small bar. Inside, customers sat at wooden tables, drinking and smoking opium. Every few minutes, one of them fell off their chair from smoking too much opium. The waiters carried them to a bed at the side of the room, and they slept.

Fix ordered wine and the two men chatted.

When the bottles were empty, Passepartout stood up.

"I must go," he said.

Fix put a hand on his arm. "Not yet. I need to tell you something."

"What is it?" asked the servant, sitting down again.

"Have you worked out who I am?"

"Yes," said the servant. "The Reform Club sent you."

"No," said Fix. "I'm a police detective."

Passepartout was amazed.

"I see that you don't know about the robbery," said Fix. "Your master stole fifty-five thousand pounds from the Bank of England. He's travelling around the world because he doesn't want the police to find him."

Passepartout jumped up. "That's not true. My master is a good man."

"If you help me, we can share the two-thousand-pound reward."

"Help you?" said the servant. "No, I'll never help you."

He tried to leave but his legs didn't feel strong enough.

"I've drunk too much," he complained.

Fix put him some opium into Passepartout's hand and he smoked it without thinking. A few minutes later, he fell under the table.

"Perfect!" said Fix. "Now Fogg won't find out that the *Carnatic* is leaving tonight."

After paying the bill, Fix left the bar while Passepartout slept.

Chapter 10

A storm at sea

While Passepartout was still sleeping in the bar, Fogg was taking Aouda around Hong Kong, looking for her uncle. But they soon found out that he wasn't there anymore.

"He left two years ago," a businessman told them. "He made a lot of money and moved to Europe."

Aouda was upset. "What can I do?"

"Come to Europe with us," Fogg said kindly.

The next morning, Passepartout wasn't at the hotel. At eight o'clock, Fogg and Aouda took a taxi to the harbour because the *Carnatic* was due to leave at half past nine.

When Fogg arrived, he didn't find his servant... or the ship.

They met Detective Fix at the harbour. Fogg was very calm while Fix explained about the ship.

"Maybe Passepartout caught the ship yesterday," said Aouda, "and he thought that we were already on it."

The next steamship to Japan wasn't leaving for a week, and that delay gave Fix time for the warrant to arrive.

But Fogg didn't want to wait. He looked across the crowded harbour and said, "There are lots of other boats here. I'm sure that one will take us to Japan."

After looking for three hours, he found a small boat called the *Tankadere*. Its captain invited them to travel with him.

"I can't take you to Yokohama," he said. "My boat is too small to travel that far. But I can take you to Shanghai, which is closer."

"That's no good," said Fogg. "I must catch the San Francisco steamship at Yokohama, not at Shanghai."

The captain smiled. "That steamship doesn't start from Yokohama. It stops there, but it starts from Shanghai."

"Are you sure?" asked Fogg.

"Yes. It leaves Shanghai on the 11th, at seven in the evening. That gives us four days."

"I'll pay you some money now," said Fogg, "and I'll give you a reward of two hundred pounds if we arrive in time."

The captain agreed. Fogg also invited Detective Fix to travel with them.

"Poor Passepartout," said Aouda sadly.

"I'll go and look for him," said Fogg. "We still have an hour before we leave."

He looked everywhere but he couldn't find his servant.

Fogg, Aouda and Fix got onto the *Tankadere* and they left the harbour.

The journey to Shanghai was more than one thousand, three hundred kilometres, and the sea was dangerous. The Chinese seas are rough and the winds are strong.

Phileas Fogg stood and looked calmly at the dark water. But Aouda was worried that the boat was too small.

But then the sky became dark and the winds became stronger.

"A storm is coming," the captain said.

He was right. At eight o'clock, a storm hit the boat. Several times, the boat nearly went under the water.

The night was terrible but, at the end of the next day, the storm was gone. Finally, the tired passengers could rest.

By noon the next day, they were only seventy kilometres from Shanghai. But they only had six hours to complete their journey and the wind was getting calmer!

Then suddenly, they saw a large ship in front of
 merican steamship for Yokohama.

 ut you!" shouted the

Fix sat quietly, thinking. Should he follow Fogg to America? He couldn't arrest him there – it wasn't a British country – but he didn't want to lose him.

For two days, the trip went. "I'm sure we'll get to Shanghai in time," the captain told Fogg.

Fix sat quietly, thinking. Should he follow Fogg to America? He couldn't arrest him there – it wasn't a British country – but he didn't want to lose him.

For two days, the trip went. "I'm sure we'll get to Shanghai in time," the captain told Fogg.

But then the sky became dark and the winds became stronger.

"A storm is coming," the captain said.

He was right. At eight o'clock, a storm hit the boat. Several times, the boat nearly went under the water.

The night was terrible but, at the end of the next day, the storm was gone. Finally, the tired passengers could rest.

By noon the next day, they were only seventy kilometres from Shanghai. But they only had six hours to complete their journey and the wind was getting calmer!

Then suddenly, they saw a large ship in front of them. It was the American steamship for Yokohama.

"It's leaving Shanghai without you!" shouted the captain.

Fogg thought for a moment. "Move closer to it. We'll climb onto it while it's moving."

It was a dangerous plan but the captain agreed. Carefully, the captain brought the *Tankadere* next to the great ship. Fogg paid him a reward of five hundred and fifty pounds, then the passengers climbed onto the ship.

A moment later, the small boat was gone and the American steamship was on the open sea.

Chapter 11

A trip to the circus

The *Carnatic* started its journey from Hong Kong to Japan at half past six on 7 November. The next day, a very tired passenger came slowly out of one of the rooms.

It was Passepartout.

After Fix left the opium bar, two waiters carried Passepartout to a bed. He slept for hours. When he finally woke up, his head hurt and he couldn't remember why he was there.

Then suddenly he remembered. "The *Carnatic*!" he shouted, jumping up.

He hurried to the harbour. The ship was leaving and he ran onto it. He found his room, lay down and slept again.

When he woke up the next morning, the *Carnatic* was already two hundred and fifty kilometres from China. Passepartout went to find his master, but the captain told him, "There is no passenger called Phileas

Fogg on this ship."

Passepartout understood immediately. "My master didn't know the time changed so he missed the ship – and it's all because of that horrible Detective Fix."

He was angry but there was nothing he could do.

On 13 November, the *Carnatic* entered the harbour of Yokohama. Passepartout got off the ship and began walking through the busy streets, looking in the shop windows. The streets were crowded with people and they wore strange clothes.

He was hungry but he had no money.

The next day, he walked again through the crowded streets. His legs were tired and he was so hungry that his stomach hurt. Then he saw a large sign:

Come and see

the Great Japanese Circus

*with funny dancers and **fake** noses!*

Passepartout stopped and smiled. "A circus! I worked for one in Paris. Maybe they will give me a job."

He followed the address on the sign and found the circus building. Inside, he spoke to manager.

"Can you sing and stand on your head at the same time?" asked the man.

"Yes!" said Passepartout.

"Good. Then you can join the show. Here are your clothes – and don't forget this fake nose."

"A fake nose?" said Passepartout, surprised.

"Yes. Everyone in our circus wears one."

Passepartout laughed. "Alright!"

At three o'clock, the show began. People from all over the world filled the seats. Men played Japanese instruments while Passepartout and the others danced.

Then suddenly Passepartout stopped moving. He saw his master in the crowd.

He forgot about the music, the dance and his fake nose. He left the other dancers and they all fell to the floor.

He ran to Fogg. "My master!" he shouted.

The circus manager was very angry but Fogg quickly gave him some money and said, "We'll take him with us."

Master, servant and Aouda went to the harbour together.

At half past six, they got onto the American steamship for San Francisco.

Chapter 12

The journey to San Francisco

Now let's go back and see what happened to Fogg, Aouda and Fix in Yokohama. They arrived early on 14 November. If Passepartout was there, they had to find him without delay – the San Francisco steamship was leaving that evening.

Fogg looked for him everywhere but couldn't find him. But he and Aouda went to see a circus show – and they found him there.

Then, together, they hurried to the harbour and caught the *General Grant*, a large steamship that could cross the Pacific Ocean in twenty-one days.

Fogg looked in his notebook and worked out the dates. "I hope we can reach San Francisco by 3 December, New York by the 11th and London by the 20th," he said calmly.

He didn't talk much, but Aouda watched him and saw how kind and intelligent he was. She was beginning to love him.

Nine days after leaving Japan, Fogg said, "We've now travelled exactly half the world. We've used fifty-two days of the total. There are twenty-eight days left."

Detective Fix was also on the ship. One morning, Passepartout saw him. He ran and hit him in the face!

"How could you leave me in that opium bar?" he shouted.

"I was trying to stop your master," Fix explained. "But now I want to help him instead."

Passepartout looked at him. "Help him? Why?"

"I finally have the warrant to arrest him but I can't use it until he arrives back in Britain. So I'll stay with him and help him to reach home."

Passepartout listened carefully but he didn't really **trust** the detective.

"If you try to stop us again, I'll break your neck!" he said.

Passepartout didn't tell Fogg that Fix was a detective. He didn't want his master to be angry or worried. Fix was helping them now, anyway.

At seven in the morning on 3 December, the *General Grant* entered San Francisco harbour. Passepartout was so excited to be in America that he tried to jump off the ship. But he jumped badly and fell into the water!

Fogg went to find out about the trains. The first one to New York was due to leave at six that evening so they had the whole day to see the city.

San Francisco was full of life, with wide streets, tall buildings and large shops that sold things from all over the world.

"It feels a very safe place," said Aouda.

"Maybe," said Passepartout. "But the trains aren't safe. There are attacks sometimes. Shall I buy some **guns**?"

"I don't think we'll need them," said Fogg. "But if you want to, here is some money."

Fogg went to get a stamp for his passport and bought some new clothes. When he met Passepartout again, the servant was carrying six guns.

At a quarter to six, the group – Fogg, Aouda, Passepartout and Fix – arrived at the station.

A minute later, the train gave a loud whistle and began its long journey across America.

Chapter 13
The broken bridge

The railway across America had two parts. The first part went from San Francisco to Omaha, through big open fields where lots of **Native Americans** lived. The second part went from Omaha to New York. In total, the railway was six thousand kilometres long.

Before the railway, the journey from San Francisco to New York took at least six months. Now, it took only seven days. Phileas Fogg hoped to reach New York by 11 December and catch the Atlantic steamship to Liverpool, England.

The train left San Francisco station at six o'clock. It was already dark, the air was cold and the clouds were heavy with snow.

Soon, snow began to fall and covered everything in white. But the train didn't stop. While the passengers slept, it hurried across California.

When morning came, the passengers looked out of the window and saw beautiful mountains and lots of wild animals.

At midday, the train suddenly stopped. A group of about ten thousand **buffalo** were slowly crossing the **track**.

Passepartout was angry and wanted to kill them with his guns.

"Why doesn't the driver do anything?" he shouted.

"He can't," Fogg said calmly. "When the buffalo are gone, he'll go faster and we won't be late."

It took hours for the last buffalo to cross the track. By that time, it was dark.

The train started moving again and soon entered Utah. At half past twelve, they reached the Great Salt Lake – more than one hundred kilometres wide. Its water is so full of salt that no fish can live in it.

This was where the Mormons lived. They built their homes here many years ago.

Later, the train went past the Rocky Mountains. The snow was heavier now and Passepartout felt worried. "If it gets any worse, we'll never reach New York," he thought. "Why did my master make this journey in winter?"

Suddenly, the train whistled and stopped.

"Why have we stopped?" asked Fix. "We're not at a station."

Passepartout jumped down and ran to the front. The

driver pointed to a wooden bridge. "We can't cross it," he said. "Parts of it are broken and the train is too heavy."

Passepartout looked and he saw that it was true. The bridge wasn't safe.

"So what are you going to do?" he asked.

"A train from Omaha is coming for us but it won't arrive for at least six hours."

"Six hours!" shouted Passepartout.

Other passengers joined the conversation and started complaining too. One man, an engineer, said, "If we go very fast, we can cross before the bridge breaks."

"That's crazy!" said Passepartout.

But the other passengers trusted the engineer and they liked his idea. The driver agreed and everyone climbed back onto the train.

It whistled loudly and began to move along the track – faster and faster – one hundred and sixty kilometres an hour.

Fogg and the others watched from the window while the broken bridge got closer and closer.

Then, with a terrible noise, the train crossed! It

almost jumped from one side of the river to the other.

As soon as the last carriage touched ground, the bridge broke and fell into the water below.

Chapter 14

The attack of the Native Americans

Three days later, Phileas Fogg was about four days from New York. The train was following the Platte River through wide, empty land. Fogg and Aouda played whist, enjoying the pleasant journey.

Then everything changed. There was shouting outside and the sound of guns. When they looked through the window, they saw about a hundred Native Americans on horses riding next to the train.

The train didn't stop. The Native Americans climbed onto it while it was moving along the track and began attacking the passengers.

It was lucky that nearly all the passengers had guns. Aouda took one of Passepartout's and used it against the Native Americans.

During the attack, three passengers died and about twenty Native Americans. Then the Native Americans rode away on their horses.

Everyone was pleased. But when Fogg looked

around, he couldn't see Passepartout.

"Where is he?" asked Aouda, starting to cry. "Did they kill him – or take him?"

No one knew.

The passengers got off the train. The carriages were

covered in blood. Far away, they could see the Native Americans.

Fogg looked at Aouda and said quietly, "I think they took Passepartout. I'll go and rescue him."

He looked at the other passengers. "You can all share five thousand dollars if you help me."

Several men agreed to join him. It was midday.

Aouda caught Fogg's arm. "You'll lose a lot of money – and the bet."

"That doesn't matter," Fogg answered. Aouda smiled.

Fix stayed with Aouda while Fogg left with the other men. The detective was very worried. "Fogg won't come back, I'm sure of it! Then I'll never be able to arrest him."

The hours passed slowly. The wind got colder.

Then the train whistled. Aouda ran to the driver.

"What is happening?" she asked.

"We can't wait any longer," he said. "We're already three hours late."

"When will another train come?" she asked.

"Tomorrow evening."

"But that's too late!" she shouted. "We must wait for Mr Fogg."

"It's impossible," said the driver.

The other passengers got back onto the train, but Aouda and Fix didn't join them. The train whistled again and then it was gone.

Night came and a snow storm began. The two of them waited without sleeping.

At last, the sun came up. It was seven o'clock.

Then, they saw Fogg. He was far away but moving nearer. With him, there were the other men and Passepartout.

When they reached her, Aouda ran to Fogg. "You rescued him!" she said. Then she took Passepartout's hands in hers.

Fogg gave the money to the men who helped him.

Passepartout looked around and saw that the train was gone. "Oh no!" he said. "I've made you late again, master."

"The next train isn't until this evening," Fix told Fogg.

Fogg just said, "Ah."

Chapter 15

Race through the snow

Phileas Fogg now had a big delay. Passepartout was so upset that he was almost crying.

Fix went to speak to Fogg. "Do you really need to be in New York on the 11th before nine in the evening?"

"Yes," answered Fogg. "The steamship leaves then for Liverpool."

"And you've lost twenty hours because of the Native Americans?" he asked.

"Yes. Before the attack, I was due to arrive in New York eleven hours before the ship left."

"I see," said Fix. "So if we leave immediately, we can still catch it. Do you want to try?"

"On foot?" asked Fogg.

"No, on a **sledge**," answered Fix. "A railway worker told me about a man with a special sledge. It has **sails** and space for five or six people."

The man's name was Mudge and he agreed to take

them.

The wind was coming from the west – perfect for Fogg – and it wasn't snowing anymore. Mudge could take them to Omaha, where they could catch a train to New York.

"We might get the lost time back," said Aouda.

"We'll reach Omaha in five hours," said Mudge.

At eight o'clock, the sledge was ready. The passengers climbed onto it and covered themselves with blankets. It was very cold.

The wind filled the sails and the sledge began to move, faster and faster, moving over the snow like a boat on water.

The air cut their faces and they couldn't speak from the cold. The sledge was travelling at sixty-five kilometres an hour.

"If nothing breaks," shouted Mudge over the wind, "we'll arrive in time."

The wind became stronger and they flew faster across the snow. Passepartout's face was red from the cold but he began to hope again. They might reach New York by the evening of the 11th, perhaps before the steamship left for Liverpool.

The land around them was empty. No villages, no stations, no people. Only wide, white fields. Sometimes, they saw big black birds and groups of

wild dogs on the snow. The animals were hungry. Passepartout kept his hand on his gun, ready to kill them if they attacked – but the sledge moved too fast. Soon, the dogs were far behind them.

At noon, Mudge was sure that they were close to Omaha but he said nothing. Half an hour later, he stopped the sledge and pointed to a roof, white with snow.

"Look. That's the station. We've arrived."

Passepartout and Fix jumped off, then helped Fogg and Aouda. Fogg gave Mudge a large reward and thanked him.

They ran to the station and there was a train, ready to leave. They climbed on and the train began to move east.

It hurried through Iowa and, during the night, crossed the Mississippi River. The next day, 10 December, at four in the afternoon, they reached Chicago.

There were still one thousand, five hundred kilometres to New York but there were lots of trains. Fogg passed from one to the other and hurried through towns with old names from Europe.

Finally, they saw the Hudson River and, at a quarter past eleven on the evening of the 11th, the train stopped at the station beside the harbour.

Fogg left the carriage and looked around. The steamship for Liverpool was gone.

Chapter 16

Fire on the sea

There were no other steamships that could take them to England. Fogg knew this from his book of timetables.

"We missed the ship because of me," Passepartout said sadly. "Now you'll lose the bet and you've spent more than seven thousand pounds. You'll be poor!"

But Fogg wasn't angry. "Let's find a hotel," he said calmly.

The next day was 12 December. Fogg had to reach London by a quarter to nine on the evening of the 21st.

Fogg went back to the harbour and walked up and down, looking looked carefully at every ship. Most only had sails, which were too slow. Then he saw a small steamship called the *Henrietta*. It was almost ready to leave.

Fogg spoke to the captain. "Where are you going?"

"To Bordeaux, in France," said the captain.

"Have you got any passengers?"

"No. This isn't a passenger ship."

"Is it fast?" asked Fogg.

"Yes, quite fast."

"Will you take us to Liverpool?"

"No," said the captain coldly.

Fogg thought for a moment. "Then will you take us to Bordeaux?"

"No, not if you pay me two hundred dollars."

"And if I pay you two thousand for each passenger?" said Fogg. "There are four of us."

The captain's eyes opened wide. "Alright," he said, amazed.

An hour later, the *Henrietta* left the harbour.

The next day at noon, a man stood at the wheel of the ship – but it wasn't the captain. No, it was Phileas Fogg. The real captain was **locked** in his room, was shouting loudly.

Why? It's very simple. Fogg wanted to go to Liverpool, not Bordeaux. So several hours after the ship left the harbour, Fogg locked the captain in his room. The ship's workers didn't stop him because Fogg paid them.

So now they were travelling to England instead of France. If there was no accident or problem, they might arrive in time.

But how could Fogg control the ship so well? Nobody knew but he was very good at it.

Fix sat and thought, "This man is amazing and so clever. And he's kind to me – he paid for me to travel with him. Why am I still following him?"

The first few days went well, then the sea became rougher and a storm began. For two days, Passepartout and Aouda were afraid. But Fogg was calm and controlled the ship well, and at last the storm passed.

On 16 December, it was day seventy-five of Fogg's journey around the world and the *Henrietta* completed half its journey across the Atlantic.

The ship's engineer came to Fogg. "We don't have enough **coal** to reach Liverpool," he said.

Fogg said nothing for a long time. Then he opened the captain's door.

"We must use all the coal," he said quietly, "and, after that, we'll burn the wooden parts of the ship."

"What?" shouted the captain. "You can't burn my

ship!"

"I'll buy it," Fogg said quietly, "for twelve thousand pounds. That way, you won't lose any money."

When the captain saw the money, he agreed.

The ship's men started taking all the wood from the ship – the beds, the chairs, the doors. They all went into the fire, instead of coal.

By 20 December, they were burning the sides of the ship. Only the metal bottom of the ship was left.

Soon they finished all the wood and the fire was getting smaller. The ship moved more slowly but it reached England at last.

At twenty minutes to twelve on 21 December, the *Henrietta* arrived in Liverpool. Fogg was just six hours from London.

When he put his foot on English ground, Fix put his hand on Fogg's arm and showed him the warrant.

"Phileas Fogg, I'm arresting you."

Chapter 17

A delay in Liverpool

Phileas Fogg was in prison.

When Fix arrested him, Passepartout tried to hit the detective but a policeman stopped him. Aouda cried – she never believed that Fogg was a robber.

And Fix? He didn't feel sure anymore. But they were in Britain again and he was just doing his job.

Fogg arrived in Liverpool at twenty minutes to twelve on 21 December. He had until a quarter to nine that evening to reach the Reform Club. That gave him nine and a quarter hours. The train to London took six hours so he still had time.

Fogg sat calmly in the small prison room. Was he angry inside? We can't be sure.

He put his watch on the table and his eyes followed the hands. He walked around the room and tried to open the door, but it was locked.

Then he sat down again and wrote in his notebook:

"21 December, Saturday, Liverpool.

80th day, 11.40am."

And he waited.

At thirty-three minutes past two, he heard a sound. The door opened. Passepartout, Aouda and Fix hurried in.

Fix spoke fast. "I'm sorry – very sorry. The real robber was arrested three days ago. You're free!"

Fogg looked into the detective's eyes and hit him hard. Fix fell to the floor.

"Well done, master!" shouted Passepartout.

Fix stayed where he was. He didn't try to hit Fogg back. He knew Fogg was right.

Fogg, Aouda and Passepartout left the prison together and took a taxi to the station.

"When is the next fast train to London?" Fogg asked.

"It left half an hour ago," said the station worker.

So Fogg ordered a special train and, at three o'clock, they left Liverpool.

They had to complete the journey in five and a half hours but there were delays. When Fogg got off the train in London, all the city's clocks showed ten minutes to nine.

"I've gone around the world and lost the bet by five minutes," he said quietly.

The next day, the neighbours in Saville Row didn't know that he was home. His doors and windows were still closed.

After that long journey, with all its problems and dangers, he lost the bet and all his money because of the detective. It was terrible!

He still had twenty thousand pounds in the bank but that now belonged to the men at the Reform Club.

Fogg gave Aouda a room in his home and they all went to bed. Fogg didn't sleep. Aouda was upset so she didn't close her eyes once. Passepartout waited all night outside his master's door.

The next day was Sunday. Fogg stayed at home.

About half past seven in the evening, he asked to speak to Aouda.

They sat near the fire and he began talking. "I'm sorry that I brought you here. Before, I was rich and I wanted to give you a part of my money. But now, I have nothing."

"Why are you sorry?" said Aouda. "You rescued me

in India and kept me safe during the long journey."

She thought for a moment then took his hand. "I trust you with my life! Shall we get married?"

Fogg looked at her and there was a light in his eyes.

"I love you!" he said. "Yes. Let's get married!"

They told Passepartout, who was very pleased.

"Go and see the priest," said Fogg. "Tell him that we want to get married tomorrow, Monday."

Passepartout ran the priest's house.

Chapter 18
Home again

Everyone heard the news that Phileas Fogg was not the robber. It was in all the newspapers. On Saturday evening, there was a big crowd outside the Reform Club and people were really excited to see the famous man.

Fogg's five friends waited for him inside the Reform Club. When the clock showed twenty minutes past eight, Andrew Stuart got up and said, "In twenty-five minutes, Mr Fogg will lose his bet."

"He's lost it already, I'm sure," said Gauthier Ralph. "He won't arrive before 8.45!"

"Wait," said Samuel Fallentin. "Fogg never arrives too soon or too late. He might get here at the last minute."

They checked the clock again. It was twenty minutes to nine.

"Five minutes more," said Stuart.

The five men looked at each other but didn't speak.

Eighteen minutes to nine.

They tried to play cards but they couldn't stop watching the clock. They heard the crowd outside.

Sixteen minutes to nine! Fogg had one more minute.

The five men stood up and counted the seconds.

At the fortieth second, nothing. At the fiftieth, still nothing.

At the fifty-fifth second, they heard a loud sound in the street.

At the fifty-seventh second, the door opened and Phileas Fogg walked in calmly, the crowd behind him.

"Here I am," he said.

Yes, Phileas Fogg was there.

Let's go back in time and explain. When Passepartout went to the priest's house, he had to wait for twenty minutes.

When he left, it was thirty-five minutes past eight. Passepartout ran home as fast as his legs could carry him.

In three minutes, he was in Saville Row again.

"What's the matter?" asked his master.

"You can't get married tomorrow."

"Why not?"

"Because tomorrow… is Sunday!"

"No, tomorrow is Monday."

"No!" said Passepartout. "Today is Saturday."

"Impossible!"

"It is!" shouted Passepartout. "You've made a mistake of one day! We arrived a whole day early but there are only ten minutes left!"

Passepartout took Fogg's arm and pulled him into the street.

Fogg didn't have time to think. They jumped into a taxi and hurried to the Reform Club. The driver almost hit two dogs and five people but they arrived in time.

The clock showed a quarter to nine when he entered the room.

"Phileas Fogg has travelled around the world in eighty days!" shouted the crowd. "He has won!"

How did such a careful man make this mistake? When he reached London, he thought that it was Saturday but it was Friday – day seventy-nine of his journey.

It's very simple.

Fogg travelled east, the same way as the Sun. Because of this, each of his days was a little shorter. So he "won" an extra day without knowing it.

He saw the Sun come up and go down eighty times,

but his friends at the Reform Club only saw it seventy-nine times.

Fogg won the bet of twenty thousand pounds but he spent nearly nineteen thousand pounds during his journey. So he only kept one thousand. But that didn't matter – he wanted to win the bet and he did!

He shared that money with Passepartout and Fix. He wasn't angry with the detective anymore.

Fogg and Aouda got married and lived together in Saville Row.

Fogg went around the world in eighty days. To do this, he used steamships, trains, taxis, sledges and elephants.

But what did he win actually?

Not money. No, he won something much better.

He found a fantastic woman, who became his wife and made him very happy.

THE END

VISIT MY WEBSITE

You will find:
- **information** about my **other books**
- **free stories**
- **free exercises** for this book
  (vocabulary exercises, comprehension exercises and notes about British culture)

   ReadStories-LearnEnglish.com

MORE STORIES

A1+ Elementary

A2 Pre-intermediate

B1 Intermediate

B2 Upper intermediate

Words from the story

against the law (phr)
not allowed by the rules of a country/place

amazed (adj)
very surprised

arrest (v)
make someone go with the police because you think they did something wrong (**arrest**, n)

bet (n)
an agreement to give money if you are wrong about something (**bet,** v)

buffalo (n)
a large wild animal with horns that lives in North America

burn (v)
destroy or damage something with fire

calm (adj)
quiet and relaxed, not angry or worried

captain (n)
the leader of a ship

carriage (n)
a vehicle pulled by horses

circus (n)
a show with acrobats, clowns and trained animals

coal (n)
a hard black rock used as fuel to make heat or energy

complain (v)
say you are not happy with something

control (v)
have power over something

detective (n)
a person who investigates crimes

due (adj)
expected to arrive at a certain time

expect (v)
think something will happen

fake (adj)
not real

fine (n)
money you must pay because you did something wrong

gun (n)
a weapon that shoots bullets and can kill people

harbour (n)
a place by the sea where ships stop and people get on or off

holy (adj)
connected with gods or religion

in time (phr)
early enough to not be late

judge (n)
a person who decides what happens to a criminal

locked (adj)
closed with a key so it cannot be opened

master (n)
a man who has power or control over others, especially over a servant

Native American (n)
a person from a group that lived in North America before Europeans arrived

opium (n)
a drug made from a poppy plant

priest (n)
a person who does religious duties (=activities)

reach (v)
arrive at a place

rescue (v)
save someone from danger

reward (n)
money or a gift given to someone for doing something good or helpful

robbery (n) the act of stealing from a person or place (**robber,** n – a person who steals)

rough (adj)
not smooth, or violent and difficult

sail (n)
a large piece of cloth on a boat that catches the wind to move it

servant (n)
a person who works in someone's home doing jobs like cooking or cleaning

sledge (n)
a low vehicle without wheels used for travelling over snow or ice

stamp (n)
a mark made on paper by pressing ink on it, for example in a passport

steamship (n)
a large boat that moves using power from very hot water vapour

suddenly (adv)
quickly and without warning

track (n)
the metal lines that a train moves on

trust (v)
believe someone is honest and will do the right thing

warrant (n)
an official paper that gives the police permission to arrest someone

whistle (n)
a high, loud sound, for example made by a person, machine or train (**whistle**, v)

work out (phr v)
find the answer to something by thinking

www.ingramcontent.com/pod-product-compliance
Lightning Source LLC
Chambersburg PA
CBHW011421070526
44584CB00026BA/3788